Brands We Know

Dairy Queen

By Sara Green

Bellwether Media • Minneapolis, MN

Jump into the cockpit and take flight with Pilot books. Your journey will take you on high-energy adventures as you learn about all that is wild, weird, fascinating, and fun!

This edition first published in 2017 by Bellwether Media, Inc.

No part of this publication may be reproduced in whole or in part without written permission of the publisher.
For information regarding permission, write to Bellwether Media, Inc.,
Attention: Permissions Department,
5357 Penn Avenue South, Minneapolis, MN 55419.

Library of Congress Cataloging-in-Publication Data

Names: Green, Sara, 1964- author.
Title: Dairy Queen / by Sara Green.
Description: Minneapolis, MN : Bellwether Media, Inc., [2017] | Series:
  Pilot: Brands We Know | Includes bibliographical references and index.
Identifiers: LCCN 2015047100 | ISBN 9781626174078 (hardcover : alk.
paper)
Subjects: LCSH: International Dairy Queen, Inc.--Juvenile literature.
| Ice cream parlors--United States--History--Juvenile literature. | Ice
cream industry--United States--History--Juvenile literature. | Fast
food restaurants--United States--History--Juvenile literature.
Classification: LCC HD9281.U54 I5445 2017 | DDC 647.9573--dc23
LC record available at http://lccn.loc.gov/2015047100

Printed in the United States of America, North Mankato, MN.

Table of Contents

What Is Dairy Queen?

The soccer team wants a treat after playing an exciting game. When the coaches suggest Dairy Queen, the players quickly agree. They cannot wait to get a Blizzard, Dilly Bar, or other delicious dessert. Choosing Dairy Queen was easy. The hard part is deciding what to order!

Dairy Queen, also known as DQ, is a **chain** of restaurants recognized for its **soft serve** desserts. Its official name is International Dairy Queen, Inc. Company **headquarters** is in Edina, Minnesota. Dairy Queen also offers hamburgers, chicken strips, and other hot foods. Orange Julius smoothies and original drinks are more **brand** favorites. Today, Dairy Queen is one of the largest fast food chains in the world. Its **logo**, shaped like a red **ellipse**, is recognized across the globe!

By the Numbers

more than
6,600
locations worldwide

35 million
customers per day

6.5 million
pounds (2.9 million
kilograms) of
strawberries
used per year

more than
$100 million
raised for Children's
Miracle Network
Hospitals since 1984

more than
30
countries with
DQ restaurants

more than
100
Blizzard flavors
introduced since
1985

more than
$4 billion
total sales
in 2014

A Cool, Creamy Idea

Dairy Queen started with an idea about a different way to serve ice cream. In the early 1930s, a man named John McCullough and his son, Alex, owned an ice cream company. They were located in Illinois. John did not like ice cream too frozen or hard. He created soft serve. It was smooth and creamy. But, he needed a way to see if others liked his new product.

The McCulloughs had a customer named Sherb Noble. He owned three ice cream **parlors** in Kankakee, Illinois. John told Sherb about his idea. Sherb agreed to do a trial sale at his store. One August day in 1938, Sherb offered a special deal. Customers could have as much soft serve as they wanted for ten cents. People packed the store. Sherb handed out more than 1,600 servings in about two hours. John's soft serve was a success!

all-you-can-eat soft serve

A Secret Recipe
The recipe for Dairy Queen's soft serve is locked in a box. Only a few people have keys!

Pictured from left to right: Sherb Noble, Alex McCullough, and friend Paul Metla at an early Dairy Queen.

In 1940, Sherb and the McCulloughs' first soft serve stand opened in Joliet, Illinois. A new freezer kept the soft serve cold but not frozen. It easily **dispensed** the treat. Sherb topped each serving with a curl! The new stand needed a name. John believed soft serve was the "queen" of dairy products. He chose the name Dairy Queen.

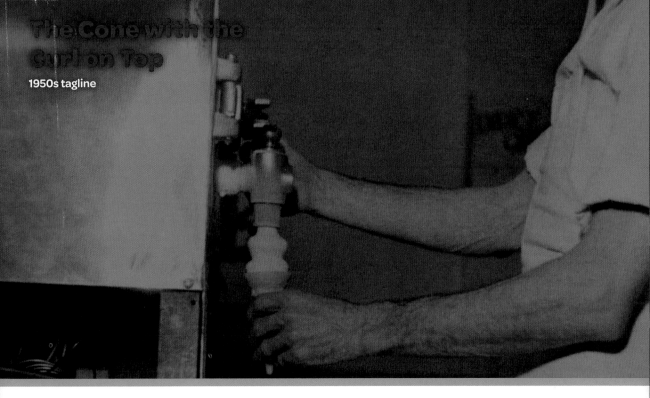

The restaurant's menu was simple. It offered sundaes and two sizes of cones. Customers could also order containers to take home. In 1949, malts and milkshakes were added to the menu. Over the next few years, many more Dairy Queen stores opened. They each had a large sign that had a soft serve cone with a curl.

Lifelong Loyalty

At the age of 82, Sherb Noble ran seven Dairy Queen stores!

The DQ Menu Expands

Dairy Queen was one of the first restaurant chains to allow **franchises**. The chain grew to 2,600 restaurants by 1955. During this time, most Dairy Queens were walk-ups and only open in warm months.

In the 1950s, banana splits and Dilly Bars became available. Sundae toppings began to include pineapple. The chain then added hamburgers, hot dogs, and other hot **brazier** foods to its menu.

Dairy Queen's headquarters moved to Minnesota in 1962. That decade saw the introduction of Mr. Misty slush treats and the Buster Bar. Over time, the look of Dairy Queen restaurants also changed. Flat roofs became slanted. The red Dairy Queen sign replaced the curly cone sign. Now, people could recognize Dairy Queen from a distance.

Brain Freeze!
The Mr. Misty slushy was renamed Arctic Rush. Its flavors include cherry, blue raspberry, and lemon lime.

Dairy Queen kept adding delicious treats to its menu. The "scrumpdillyishus" Peanut Buster Parfait was introduced in the 1970s. Vanilla soft serve, peanuts, and fudge made this treat extra yummy.

In 1985, Dairy Queen introduced the Blizzard. Candy, cookies, and other items are blended with soft serve to make these desserts. They are thick enough to serve upside down. The Blizzard helped make Dairy Queen the top treat chain in the United States. The restaurant sold more than 175 million Blizzards in the first year!

Blizzard

Peanut Buster Parfait

We Treat You Right
1980s-1990s tagline

A World Record
A Canadian DQ made the largest ice cream cake in the world in 2011. It weighed nearly 22,334 pounds (10,130 kilograms)!

Oreo is one of the most popular Blizzard flavors. M&M's and Strawberry Cheesecake are other favorites. Dairy Queen also offers Blizzard of the Month. These special flavors include Candy Cane Oreo and Pumpkin Pie. Today, the Blizzard is the best-selling dessert at Dairy Queen.

Dairy Queen continued to grow and change. The company bought Karmelkorn in 1986. A year later, Dairy Queen bought the Orange Julius chain. It makes **frothy** juices and fruit smoothies. Flavors include orange, strawberry, and mango pineapple. Eventually, Dairy Queen added Orange Julius drinks to all its menus across North America.

So Good, It's RiDQulous

2010s tagline

14

In 1998, Dairy Queen was bought by a large business called Berkshire Hathaway. The chain then launched DQ Grill & Chill restaurants in **urban** areas soon after. The restaurants were large and had comfortable dining rooms. New menu choices included breakfast items, grilled sandwiches, salads, and self-serve soft drinks. In 2015, customers began enjoying DQ Bakes. These oven-baked foods include sandwiches and hot desserts **à la mode**. Dairy Queen also changed its kids' drink menu. Instead of soda, it offers milk or water.

DQ Around the World

People around the world enjoy DQ food and treats. About 30 countries have Dairy Queen restaurants. China alone has around 700 locations. The world's largest Dairy Queen is in Saudi Arabia. It is two stories and seats 240 people.

DQ menus around the world are similar. They often include hamburgers, hot dogs, and fries. Blizzards are also popular. Some countries offer unique flavors. In Poland, candy-filled Lion Bar Blizzards are favorites. Green Tea Blizzards are top sellers in many Asian countries. They can come with red beans, bananas, almonds, or chocolate chunks. In Thailand, customers can order Mango Blizzards topped with sticky rice.

A Lone Star Favorite

In the United States, Texas has more than 570 Dairy Queen locations. They even have their own items like "The Dude" and "Hungr-Buster."

Beijing, China

Blizzard Flavors Around the World

Country	Flavor
Canada	Birthday Cake Oreo
China	Durian
Guyana	Pine Tart
Indonesia	Green Tea Banana
Mexico	Mango Cheesecake
Panama	Strawberry Oreo
Poland	Lion Bar
Saudi Arabia	Mango Coconut
Thailand	Mango Sticky Rice
Trinidad and Tobago	Coconut Waffle Crisp

Dairy Queen in Doha, Qatar

Helping Kids Smile

Dairy Queen has been a **sponsor** of Children's Miracle Network Hospitals since 1984. DQ owners in the U.S. and Canada hold special events to raise money. Many DQs participate in Miracle Treat Day. Each restaurant gives some of the money from Blizzard sales to local hospitals. Sometimes, celebrities help promote the day. Over time, this event and others like it have helped Dairy Queen donate more than $100 million to hospitals.

DQ gives back to kids in other ways. Every year, the chain gives Dilly Bars to some Minnesota organizations that help kids in need. Dairy Queen also aided a Wisconsin police department. The police gave children DQ treats for safe behavior. If kids wore their helmets or seatbelts, they would get a Dilly Bar coupon. Dairy Queen's treats bring sweetness to people every day!

Marie Osmond promoting Miracle Treat Day

NHL player David Clarkson helping with
Miracle Treat Day

Dairy Queen Timeline

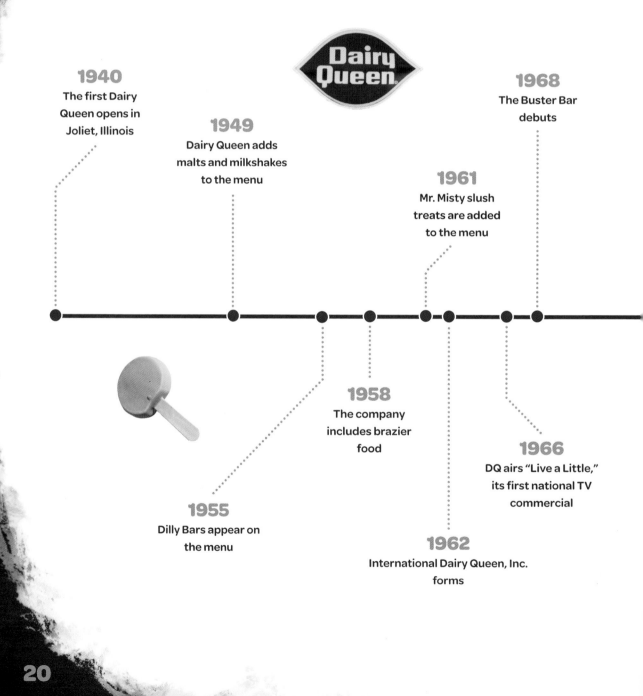

1940
The first Dairy Queen opens in Joliet, Illinois

1949
Dairy Queen adds malts and milkshakes to the menu

1968
The Buster Bar debuts

1961
Mr. Misty slush treats are added to the menu

1958
The company includes brazier food

1955
Dilly Bars appear on the menu

1966
DQ airs "Live a Little," its first national TV commercial

1962
International Dairy Queen, Inc. forms

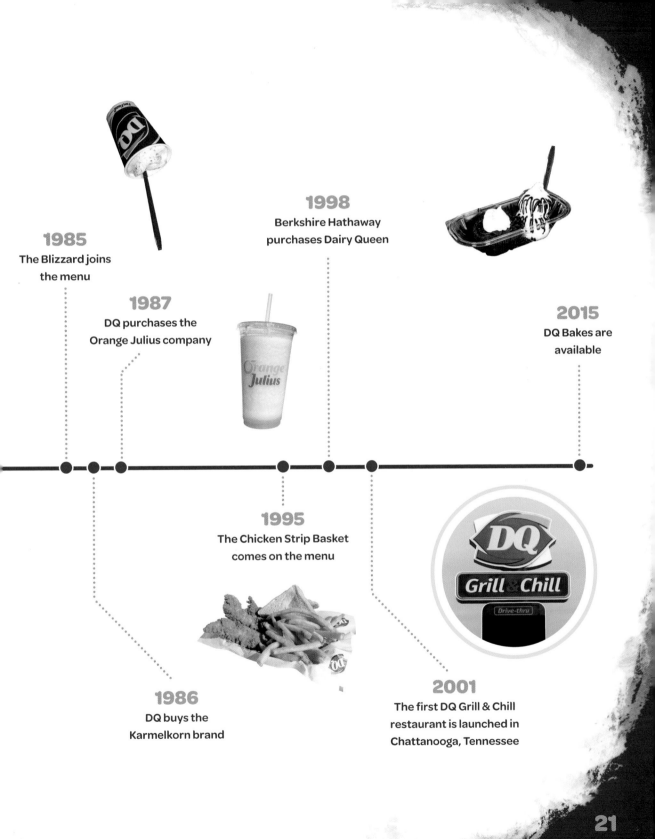

1985
The Blizzard joins
the menu

1987
DQ purchases the
Orange Julius company

1998
Berkshire Hathaway
purchases Dairy Queen

2015
DQ Bakes are
available

1995
The Chicken Strip Basket
comes on the menu

1986
DQ buys the
Karmelkorn brand

2001
The first DQ Grill & Chill
restaurant is launched in
Chattanooga, Tennessee

Glossary

à la mode—comes with soft serve

brand—a category of products all made by the same company

brazier—a pan or stand that holds hot coals for grilling

chain—a set of related restaurants or businesses with the same name

dispensed—gave out in portions

ellipse—an oval shape

franchises—restaurants or businesses operated by people only after they receive permission from a company that owns the rights to the restaurant or business

frothy—foamy

headquarters—a company's main office

logo—a symbol or design that identifies a brand or product

parlors—small stores or businesses

soft serve—smooth, soft ice cream made in and dispensed from a freezer in which it is constantly churned and combined with air

sponsor—a person or organization that gives money to others for a project or activity in return for being able to promote their brand

urban—relating to cities and city life

To Learn More

AT THE LIBRARY

Cornell, Kari A. *Dandy Desserts*. Minneapolis, Minn.: Millbrook Press, 2014.

Green, Sara. *Hershey's*. Minneapolis, Minn.: Bellwether Media, 2015.

Mattern, Joanne. *Ben & Jerry: Ice Cream Manufacturers*. Minneapolis, Minn.: ABDO Pub., 2015.

ON THE WEB

Learning more about Dairy Queen is as easy as 1, 2, 3.

1. Go to www.factsurfer.com.

2. Enter "Dairy Queen" into the search box.

3. Click the "Surf" button and you will see a list of related web sites.

With factsurfer.com, finding more information is just a click away.

Index

The images in this book are reproduced through the courtesy of: Jon Eppard, front cover (all), pp. 4 (all), 10 (top), 12 (right), 20 (bottom), 21 (top middle, bottom); Ivansabo, (table of contents), p. 21 (right); kevin brine, p. 5 (building); KZww, p. 5 (sky); The Noble Family, pp. 6, 7, 8, 9 (top); Pinkcandy, p. 9 (bottom); Library of Congress/ Getty Images, p. 10 (bottom); car culture/ Getty Images, p. 11; Josh Brink, p. 12 (right), 21 (top left); Greig Reekie/ Newscom, p. 13 (top); Richard Levine/ Age Fotostock, p. 13 (bottom); ZUMA Press/ Alamy, p. 14; Ken Wolter, p. 15; RosalreneBetancourt 5/ Alamy, p. 16; Bob Martin/ Getty Images, p. 17; AR4 WENN Photos/ Newscom, p. 18; Rick Madonik/ Getty Images, p. 19; jackbluee, p. 20 (top); Glen Stubbe/ ZUMA Press, p. 21 (middle right).